Mobilizing Local Ministries Series

Every Believer Redeemed for Global Harvest

Six Primary Roles to Involve Your Whole Ministry

Every Believer Redeemed for Global Harvest.
By Joel Iyorwa

Published by IGNITE Media
GMMI
100 County Rd. 263
Armstrong, MO 65230
www.GlobalMMI.net

First Print 2020, Copyright 2021 by IGNITE Media
All Rights Reserved

ISBN: 978-1-956435-14-6

All Scripture quotations are taken from the New King James Version. Copyright 1982, Thomas Nelson,Inc.

Cover Design - Bew Kanokkan Puranawit
Formatting Design - Acts Company, Chiang Mai, Thailand

More copies of this writing can be ordered from www.GlobalMMI.net or by contacting info@GlobalMMI.net

Joel Iyorwa can be personally contacted at jiyorwa@globalmmi.net.

Chapter I.
Every Believer Has A Role To Play

The phrase "Every Believer has a role to play" sounds simple enough, but in the current climate of the Church, it is a radical, if not revolutionary claim. A lot of believers today agree to some extent, that the Church of Jesus needs to be active in cross-cultural missions or world evangelization. But this partial consensus has come with a caveat – God has called some people in the church with a special calling to Missions, and it is their job to carry out the Great Commission.

In other words, while a lot of Believers think it is important to evangelize all the nations of the world, most of them don't think it involves them personally, that they are also called to participate in the task of World Evangelization. Even among those who accept that the call to missions isn't just for a few professionals categorized as missionaries, that conviction (if we can call it that) is [often] merely theological and not practical.

Two hundred years ago, the church completely denied the task of missions or world evangelization. They argued that the church does not need to send missionaries anywhere or actively seek to evangelize the world because if God desires to save any "heathen tribes" around the world, he would do so with his omnipotent and omnipresent power without any help from man. Those who tried to buck the trend and go against the theological tide of the day were not only opposed, they were often called heretics and became outcasts.

But as the Church began to shift from this extreme theological position, it quickly embraced another extreme – only some people, a small group of gifted and specially called people were to take on the responsibility.

They were called missionaries. From William Carey to Hudson Taylor to Rowland Bingham, a small handful of people have carried the burden while most others have looked on and merely cheered their bravery and sacrifice. This line of thinking persists today among large swaths of believers, churches and fellowships.

This is the new paradigm that needs to shift today. The church needs to move away from the Missionaries-only or some-believers-only mentality to the conviction that God wants every believer to be involved, to participate in the fulfilment of the Great Commission, in reaching the unreached and raising committed followers of Jesus Christ in every distinct people group of the world.

It is neither true that God will save the unreached unilaterally without the labor of men (although He could) nor is it true that only a few professionals (who often give up everything to serve full time as missionaries, church planters, evangelists, pastors and so on), are shouldered with the responsibility of world evangelization.

The radical idea here is that every believer, including – if not especially – those with so called 'secular professions', who may not be necessarily serving in full time missionary roles or Church-related careers and ministries, are also called to participate, nonetheless. The medical doctors and nurses, engineers and pilots, Bankers and architects, Businessmen/women and politicians, students and the unemployed, have an equal stake and calling as the missionary – the workers who leave everything behind to cross the seas and oceans and plant churches. Every believer has a role to play, no matter who they are or what they are doing with their life.

The Real Possibility of Fulfilling the Great Commission In Our Lifetime.

There was a time when the idea of "finishing" or "completing" the task of Mission – Making disciples out of every people group and tribe on earth – sounded preposterous, even impossible. Even as recently as a century ago, even those who were at the forefront of the Missions enterprise didn't or couldn't fathom any possibility of fulfilling the Great Commission and finishing the task of world evangelization.

But Since the turn of the 21st century, a surge of interest has been focused on "finishing the task," "completing the task of evangelizing the world," and "fulfilling the Great Commission." Entire conferences and strategic think tanks have been held with these themes since then. More and more people are suddenly realizing that the Great Commission or the task of evangelizing the whole world is doable in our lifetime.

Such a newfound optimism and enthusiasm isn't unfounded. The reasons for this are not farfetched. For starters, we have a thousand percent times more believers today and incredibly far less unreached people groups today than when the Great Commission was first given. Here's some actual numbers: In AD 100, there were 360 Unreached Peoples for every single believer, but today, there are just 7.3 Unreached Peoples for every believer. Furthermore, there were twelve Unreached Peoples for every congregation of believers, but today, there is only one Unreached People for every 1000 congregation.

Another reason to feel optimistic and hopeful about the literal fulfilment of the Great Commission today, aside from the greater numbers of believers and fewer numbers of the unreached, is the unprecedented advancement in technology at our disposal today and the rapid globalization that has been taking place for the last fifty years or so. Whilst William Carey and Hudson Taylor (both pioneer missionaries to the unreached) took months to sail from England to India and China respectively, those same trips today would take just a few hours, to state just one of many incredible examples of the advantages we face today.

The One Problem Stopping Us Today

While it is true today, that we live at a time in history when the literal fulfillment of the Great Commission to "go into all the world and make disciples of all nations" no longer seems like a distant reality, and despite the unprecedented technology and advancement in modern life today, fulfilling the Great Commission largely remains just a dream. Billions remain unreached, and millions remain unengaged. Many of these unreached and unengaged don't even know any follower of Jesus personally, have never talked with one, and have never seen or heard from the Bible and so have very little hope of ever hearing a culturally relevant gospel in their lifetime.

The one thing most desperately lacking in all our effort to reach the unreached today, isn't necessarily money or equipment or strategy, but the fact that too few believers are involved, or the fact that most believers are not involved, and only a few are left to grapple with the enormous harvest fields of unreached peoples. It has been reported for instance that only "1 in 20,000 believers go to evangelize the unreached", and 70% of believers today don't even know about the state of the unreached who need to hear the gospel.

There is indeed cause to believe that the situation would be different if EVERY BELIEVER was operating consciously in their God given roles at home or out on the field in the Great Commission. Too few people are currently involved – it is often left to a small number of "professionals" whose job it is thought to be to evangelize the world. But every believer has a role. The call to disciple all nations is not just for a few Christians but every member of the body of Christ irrespective of status, background, education, etc.

What are those roles? How can we identify and fulfill those roles effectively? Why are we not all operating in our different roles? These are questions we want to answer here. Pastors of local churches and leaders of ministries also have the responsibility to guide and influence those under their care to discover and play their own individual roles. Imagine what would happen if every member of your church, ministry or campus fellowship was actively playing their roles.

Traditionally, we talk of Four different kinds of Great Commission roles: Praying, Going, Sending, and Mobilizing. However, the roles available to all believers now include two more that are typically referred to as Welcoming and Advocating. Every believer can be involved in one or more of these roles. They are not to be understood as mutually exclusive roles. One cannot say, for instance, "I'm a mobilizer, so I don't need to give (send)." Believers should be involved to some extent in all or as many of the roles as possible and as opportunities are available, but they also should prayerfully determine what is the consistent role they must commit themselves to long-term and be dedicated to.

Chapter II.

Sending

(Giving & Supporting Those Who Go in Various Ways)

Senders are those who make it physically and logistically possible for message bearers to go and remain in active service on the field. Sending is not just about enabling people to go, but, more crucially, enabling and empowering them to stay. For message bearers to go and stay, many things are necessary, and several support mechanisms need to be in place to make it work.

Those actions happening to make going to the unreached and staying (sustenance) possible add up to what we refer to as Sending, and the individuals behind those efforts are those we call Senders. Elsewhere in this handbook, sending as a local church or corporate body will be discussed, but here the focus is on sending as an individual role for believers in the Great Commission. Sending and senders are important links in the Great Commission chain of actors and actions. While much of sending has to do with financial support, it is by no means limited to finances alone. It is much more than just writing the checks.

Not withstanding, giving is one of the most essential aspects of sending, which is why the terms giving and sending can be used interchangeably to mean one and the same thing. A sender is also often referred to by some as a "supporter" or "partner," but the term sending captures the essence of this important role best. God has chosen not to make money grow on trees or fall like dew from the skies for His message bearers (although He could do that). All the silver and gold are His (Haggai 2:8), and He even owns the cattle on a thousand hills (Psalm 50:10). Yet, He provides for His work through His children who willingly give.

In every local church or ministry, God wants to see certain people set themselves apart and commit to faithful and sacrificial giving, people who consider themselves Kingdom treasurers, as it were. Playing the role of a sender and giving is more than just giving offerings and tithes in church. It is a strategic role and responsibility. It is not just about parting with loose change in our pockets, but giving sacrificially, not out of convenience.

A. Some Reasons for Sending

There are many reasons why the role of sending or giving is vital to the missions movement. We cannot overemphasize it; in fact, we should only be afraid of underemphasizing it.

1. It is God's expectation.

2. It is God's method.

3. Money is the single most common factor causing attrition among serving message bearers or delaying potential ones from going to serve.

4. It provides a viable way of being actively involved in the Great Commission when it is not possible to go.

5. It is the most effective way to faithfully manage our God-given resources and to invest it in eternally meaningful ways.

6. It brings heavenly joy and fulfillment.

7. It offers discipline and protection against greed and selfishness.

8. Giving in this way brings us increase and blessing as well. "It is more blessed to give than to receive."

B. Why Aren't [More] People Giving?

1. Small and selfish ambitions: Too many people are thinking only about themselves, their own immediate family and benefit. Jesus said, "Seek ye first the kingdom of God and all these [other] things shall be added unto you" (Matt. 6:33). But many people are often guilty of seeking self and family first and giving God their leftovers.

2. Ignorance: Perhaps not too many can claim ignorance as an excuse for not being a giver to the cause of the Great Commission. Still, there is a good number who need to be educated and exposed to the plethora of giving opportunities available. The ignorance is both theological (Lack of knowledge of what God's Word says about it) and Practical (lack of knowledge of the facts, information about the state of the world and it's unreached peoples).

3. Lack of motivation and example by the local church: Many Christians have grown up in churches where all they have been taught about giving to God is tithes and offerings to their local church and the pastors. Some are even discouraged outright from giving to causes outside their immediate church projects and are made to perceive this as a lack of loyalty to the local church, or even a disregard to God's principles.

4. The nothing-to-give syndrome: Perhaps more people are hindered by this than most other reasons for failing to be involved in missions as givers. People find it a convenient excuse to say "I don't have" or "I don't have enough" to give. However, this is the greatest myth about giving that ensnares believers.

Everyone has something to give. Everyone can give. The problem often lies with the heart rather than the wallet or checkbook. The conviction about giving is weak, and the passion about the Great Commission and the urgency of the task and need is lacking. Also, many people think giving to the Great Commission is all about writing four- or five-figure checks. No! The most important thing about giving is first of all the heart behind it and faithfulness, not the amount (remember the poor widow in Luke 21:1-4). God doesn't expect anyone to give beyond their means. A poor student who gives cheerfully and faithfully $2 every month is better than the rich businessman who may occasionally drop a $500 gift from his millions and doesn't even have a heart-level engagement.

5. Personal greed and materialism: The natural inclination in everybody is to always want more, to accumulate and to self-aggrandize. This makes people want to hoard and simply amass wealth. It also extends to the issue of materialism, which has become a modern-day form of idolatry. We always want a better car, the latest model of gadgets, the newest fashions, and a   better vacation experience. We fail to see the need to cut back or cut down on acquisitions and expenses in order to make funds available for God's work.

C. Other Ways to Be a Sender

1. Adopt specific individuals, teams, fields, projects or an organization. Impact is better sustained and much higher with consistent, faithful giving rather than haphazard, inconsistent giving. Prayerfully and thoughtfully adopt based on areas of greatest need and the freedom of being led by the Lord.

2. Join an existing sending (Great Commission supporters) group, fellowship or create one. Usually, such a group meets at a convenient time and place regularly (weekly, monthly, or bimonthly) to encourage each other, pray for Great Commission missionaries and their work, review missionary newsletters, reports, emails, etc. The Bible says, "two are better than one" (Eccl. 4:9-10). Together as a group or team, consider different ways to stand with the Great Commission and message bearers.

3. Connect with a message bearer(s), befriend them and develop communications with them through email, Skype, telephone, etc. However, care must be taken when communicating with message bearers in closed and hostile nations so as to not put them in danger of unnecessary and avoidable persecution or even deportation.

4. Host re-entering missionaries (message bearers) who are returning home on furlough or emergency situations, for instance. You can have them over at your house for meals or to stay in your guest room or book a resort/hotel/guesthouse for them and let them borrow your car.

5. Be an advocate for their work and needs. You might want to talk with your pastor about inviting the message bearer to speak at your church/fellowship. This would raise awareness in the congregation and possibly secure some donors and/or partners who would support them.

6. As a sender, you don't have to only operate from the comfort zone of your home and city. You can even plan and carry out physical visits to the field in order to see firsthand the environment and the ministries the Message Bearers are doing.

Chapter III.

Praying/Interceeding

Intercessors, people who dedicate themselves to the role of praying for Great Commission missionaries (message bearers) and the unreached, are vital to the fulfillment of the Great Commission. Many people often make the mistake of assuming that prayer is the easiest and most convenient role to play and so are quick to opt for the role of intercessor. However, such people very quickly realize they are not being faithful to the commitment they made; they are hardly praying at all as they realize it is easier said than done.

Intercession is a very serious responsibility and one never to be taken up lightly or casually. It is a spiritually sensitive role that should only be engaged by a very serious commitment and dedication. At the same time, it is not a complex role requiring any form of expertise necessarily, just the passion and burden to pray. Anyone can pray! But it takes good discipline to be committed, consistent and faithful.

A. The Necessity of the Role of Prayer and Intercessors

Prayer is the key, the engine room, the core of every effective spiritual work. No real, lasting and substantial spiritual work has ever been done, nor will ever be done, without prayer. The Old Testament gives us a very graphic illustration of the role of intercession in the story of Moses up on the mountain with Aaron and Hur while Joshua was down in the valley fighting the enemy. Moses and his friends were praying for Joshua and his soldiers, symbolized by Moses lifting up his hands to God. Each time Moses' arms got weary and he dropped them, the enemy would immediately begin to gain the upper hand, but each time he held his hands up, Joshua and Israel would start to win. Consequently, Aaron and Hur helped Moses to sit on a rock and each held up one arm of Moses until Joshua completely destroyed the enemy (see the entire story in Exodus 17, specifically verse 12). This story demonstrates what happens both when prayer is being made and when it is not being made. Breakthrough is impossible without dedicated prayer and intercession.

B. How to be a Great Commission Intercessor

1. It is most effective to Adopt and focus on a specific place, people group, message bearer, work and organization rather than haphazard, random and inconsistent. Still, spontaneous and more general praying is important as well. Ask God for whom or where he might have you pray. Talk with different stakeholders to ascertain where the need is greatest. Search your own heart to find where your deep-seated passion and burden lie.

2. Acquire information from and about those you are praying for. This can be done, for instance, by subscribing to email updates, blogs from message bearers and organizations, or from a regularly updated website. Information and specific prayer requests also can be obtained through email and Skype/phone communications.

3. Both general and specific information for Great Commission praying also can be found at the very informative website of Joshua Project and from the wonderful global prayer resource, Operation World.

4. Join a Great Commission or Global Prayer Team or start one yourself. This could be a group of anywhere between 3-10 Christians meeting regularly for updates and prayer for Great Commission missionaries (message bearers) and interceding for the unreached. During such meetings, testimonies, reports and prayer letters from message bearers are read, the Scriptures are shared, etc., to stir up prayer in an informed manner.

5. Set time aside deliberately for dedicated and consistent prayer. Being an intercessor should not be something crafted by convenience but by a strong consecration and sense of commitment.

6. Prayer walks/journeys: This is a popular way to engage in the Great Commission through prayer and intercession. It usually involves physically walking over a given location and praying over it and for it in the process or just traveling to an unreached people group to pray on-site for a certain period of time. Many people who do this have God's promise to Moses and Joshua in mind: "Every place that the sole of your foot will tread upon I have given you" (Deut. 11:24, Joshua 1:3).

C. Benefits of Praying for the Great Commission and Message Bearers

1. You are transformed into a global Christian with a global vision.

2. The joy and satisfaction of knowing that, through prayer, you are breaking fallow grounds and causing doors to open over the hard and hostile environment of unreached people groups.

3. As you pray over the issues surrounding God's heartbeat, you inevitably fall more in love with Jesus and care more about the unreached who have never been told about Him.

4. You can touch and affect the world tremendously, even the remotest parts of it, on your knees.

5. Sharing in the blessings through fruitfulness on the field and nations being turned to God.

Chapter IV.

Mobilizing

A mobilizer is someone who "sounds the rallying call," someone who works to see many other people get involved in the Great Commission in order to find their roles. They help other believers develop a Great Commission vision and a heart for the Great Commission. Sometimes, this means working to see more and more believers recruited, trained, equipped and sent out as message bearers or take up other active roles in the Great Commission.

Mobilizing others toward involvement in God's global purpose is one of the most exciting and strategic activities in which to be involved. In fact, Ralph Winter of the U.S. Center for World Mission once said that mission mobilization is the most strategic role in the missionary movement and jokingly referred to those who "lost the vision and went to the field."

A. Who Should Be a Mobilizer?

1. Passionate, global Christians who are Great Commission-minded, who have themselves caught the Great Commission vision, and who are firm believers in the necessity and urgency of the task of fulfilling the Great Commission are the ideal mobilizers. One of the prominent principles in the New Testament is that "you cannot give what you don't have." Peter said to the lame man by the beautiful gate "such as I have, I give unto you" (Acts 3:6).

2. Those who have sensed the call to go but are still at home either in school or going through various stages of preparations also can

be mobilizers. Well-known missionary and martyr Jim Elliot was a student at Wheaton College when he felt called of God to go. However, since he was still a student he couldn't go just yet, so he set out mobilizing others right there on campus.

3. Serving message bearers who are engaged on the field also can serve as mobilizers as they interact and mingle with the national church in those places where they are serving. They can motivate others through their own example and mentoring for them.

B. What is the End Goal of Mobilization?

Many people wrongly think that the end goal of mobilization is to get everyone or as many people as possible to leave what they are already doing in order to go to the field as a message bearer (missionary). This is a lopsided understanding of the role of mobilization. Instead, the end goal or objective is to help people, first of all, to have a Great Commission vision, a global understanding of God's purposes, and a passion for the lost and the fulfillment of the Great Commission.

Secondly, mobilization aims to help everyone identify their own specific, individual, God-given role in the task of the Great Commission. It is not about making people go but helping them find out how and where they can best be effective contributing to the global purposes of God in bringing the unreached to the knowledge of Christ. Going is certainly one possibility and perhaps needs to be given precedence, but there are other roles, too, as we have enumerated here. Successful mobilization gets someone to the point where he or she successfully answers the question, "What has God called me to do in order to help fulfill the Great Commission?" Mobilization exists because the Great Commission doesn't. The whole purpose of mobilization is that of action – connecting people to their most strategic role in completing the Great Commission.

C. Ways of Mobilizing:

1. Prayer: Get people praying for the Great Commission! Prayer is one of the most effective ways to receive a heart-level impartation of global mission vision.

2. Study the Bible: God's Word is one of the greatest mobilization tools. Again, small groups could be formed to study about God's heart for the nations and God's provisions in Scripture for the unreached.

3. Spread or share Great Commission information: It has been said, "Information is power!" Without information, the morale for action is often lacking.

4. Training courses/seminars: Training Courses and Seminars are also a powerful way to mobilize people. There are many good courses offered all over the world today. Some provide entry-level information, others more advanced information. Examples include the Perspectives on the World Christian Movement course. GMMI (Formerly known as SVM2) also has several very good training programs and courses, including the Great Commission Seminar. More information available at globalgmmi.net. A mobilizer can personally take these courses as well as plan and organize them to be held in the local church or campus.

Chapter V.

Going

"GO YE into all the world and preach the gospel to every creature"
Mark 16:15.

"...And how shall they hear without a preacher" Romans 10:14.

The most direct role in the Great Commission is doing just what it says to do – go! Goers are the people who have identified their role in the Great Commission as frontier cross-cultural workers. "Goers" often have to make a number of sacrifices and typically give up the life they have always known, leave their comfort zones, leave behind family and friends or careers, long-held dreams and ambitions in order to go and live in a new culture and among an unreached people group. They often must learn a new language as well so that they can be a witness to the Gospel among such people. It may last anywhere from several months to a lifetime. Unless some believers are willing and committed to actually going, nothing will happen to bring the unreached to Jesus, no matter how much we passionately pray or how generously we give or how creatively we mobilize.

A. Why Go?

There are still around 2.48 billion people in the world today who are considered unreached with the Gospel. They make up 41.3% of the world's population. These are not just statistics but real people, entire people groups, huge swaths of entire countries who have no Christians, no church and no Bible and absolutely no conceivable opportunity within their reach and means to hear about the love and Gospel of Jesus Christ.

The Bible asks a poignant question: "…How shall they hear without a preacher?" People like these are part of the irresistible reasons why going is hugely important. To make matters worse, the ratio of current UPG (unreached people group) workers (message bearers serving among the unreached) to the total population of the unreached world is: One missionary for every 278,431 people. This means the number of missionaries who go to reach the unreached is so small that every one of them faces the huge and impossible task of evangelizing more than a quarter of a million people.

Jesus Himself identified the solution to this plentiful harvest to be "more laborers" going. He asked us to "pray the Lord of the harvest to send more laborers" (Matthew 9:38). According to statistics by The Traveling Team, there are 95,000 evangelical Christians for every one unreached people group. If just a small number of these people would heed the call to go to the unreached and take up this role, much progress would be made in a short time toward evangelizing the remaining unreached peoples of the world.

Here are a few more reasons it's important to go:

1. The Lamb Is Worthy: Through the cross, Jesus earned the highest place of honor above every other honor possibly given. He is worthy of our best efforts and highest sacrifice, of our complete obedience, and of the worship of those who presently might be hostile toward Him or do not even know Him.

2. The Spirit Is Moving: The greatest ingathering into God's Kingdom all over the world is happening now. Current estimates put the number of people daily being added to the body of Christ worldwide averaging 174,000, with 3,500 new churches opening every week. More laborers are needed for the harvest.

3. The Lost Are Dying: Every day, more than 66,000 people die in areas where the Gospel has never taken root around the world, many having never heard it at all. They are not just dying, they are perishing.

4. The Poor Are Suffering: The spiritually and materially poor around the world are in desperate need of the holistic gospel to defeat sin and heal and restore.

5. The Church Is Commissioned to GO: As Hudson Taylor said, "The Great Commission is not an option to be considered; it is a command to be obeyed."

6. Unless We GO, We Will Lose Our Own Vitality: Going is the only way the Church stays healthy and fulfills its purpose. A healthy church is not a large church but a sending church; its spiritual health is indicated not by how many people attend its services but by how many people are being sent.

7. The Father Is Waiting: The father is obviously waiting…waiting for the Church to take the Gospel to the whole world, waiting for all nations to be given an opportunity to know and follow Jesus.

8. God is counting on us: God has a self-imposed limitation; He can but will not act by Himself, on His own, to cause the nations to know Him. He has given humanity free will to choose Him and act on His behalf to bring people into His Kingdom.

B. Why Some People Do Not GO!

But why are so few people going? Available statistics show only one out of every 20,000 believers go to the unreached. Why isn't it higher? There are several reasons why the number is so abysmally low. They include:

1. The "I'm-not-called" Mindset": This is an extremely common excuse. Bob Hughes poses the question, "Why wait for a call when you have a command?". Often, when people talk about a "call" they are referring to something mystical and fancy, like an angel appearing to them, and telling them in angelic voice to go to a certain place. This is not a very healthy idea of what a call is. While it is true that sometimes, some among us get such a dramatic and supernatural experience, it is in fact the exception, and not in any way, the norm. More than 90% of us will never see or hear an angel in that way.

But that doesn't mean we are not called. A Call is primarily a spirit-led burden and conviction in our hearts to do a certain thing. God doesn't often call people to do things that they are not already distressed in their hearts about.

2. **Cultural and family barriers:** Expectations from family and relatives and certain cultural norms hold many people back from going. Becoming a message bearer is seen as a betrayal or lack of care and concern for parents and family.

3. **Selfish ambitions:** We are naturally inclined to be highly ambitious. Often, these ambitions are driven by underlying pride and selfishness and are heavily related to societal norms and standards of living, not to biblical ideals and God's purposes.

4. **Financial constraints:** God is not financially constrained, but the goer must be willing to step out in faith, into the unknown, and trust Him to supply. Many find this too risky or inconvenient.

5. **Misunderstanding or ignorance about the Great Commission:** Some see the Great Commission as synonymous with poverty and suffering, others simply do not know what it means and so feel satisfied doing other good things in the name of missions.

C. Some Ways to Go

1. Career Missionary: Go long-term. Spend anywhere from 3-5 years and upwards in a different culture among the unreached doing a specific kind of ministry - church planting, Bible translation, etc.

2. Be a "finisher." People in their late 40s or 50s are choosing to spend their second career on the field, after ending a different career.

3. Go for a medium two-year term. Most mission agencies have an option for "medium-term" goers.

4. Go on a short-term mission trip, through a mission agency or your church. However, short-term trips are never meant to replace a long-term approach. They are more effective as part of a vision-discerning

process or as a way of gaining useful, practical cross-cultural exposure and experience.

5. Tent-Making/Business As Mission (BAM): Use your job, skill, business, degree, etc., to share the Gospel among the nations. These kinds of missionaries do not even need to deal with the extra concern of support-raising. Their careers or businesses earn them the money they need to keep up, benefit their community and earn legitimacy in the eyes of the nationals while being light and salt in the community.

6. Be a non-residential missionary. People who choose this path travel back and forth to a specific unreached place, especially when direct access is not feasible.

Chapter VI.

Advocating

Advocacy has not been talked about very much in the Great Commission enterprise today as a role. Generally, an advocate is someone who speaks on behalf of another, usually with the aim of creating a positive appeal about someone or something.

Pastor Jerry Harding of Advancing Native Mission has described advocacy as "the act of pleading for someone else, defending or standing up for someone else's cause, speaking out for those without a voice, interceding on behalf of another, bridging the gap between the need and the supply, linking hands of hurt with hands of help, connecting servants with sources, love that acts and faith that works, the natural expression of eyes that have seen, ears that have heard, and hearts that have been broken"

Great Commission advocates can sometimes speak about the unreached, becoming a voice for them, often highlighting the plight of a specific people, a special need, or a forgotten or ignored area needing attention, and then seek to generate interest and practical involvement. They can also act as communications link between frontier missions or Message Bearer Teams and the Church or Believers at home, putting the problem and needs of the unreached in the front and center of the life of the church.

Some people confuse advocacy with mobilization. This confusion is not completely without basis, for there are some similarities between the two roles. But while mobilization focuses on envisioning, educating and equipping believers for mission, advocacy goes a step further and focuses not just on inspiring and envisioning believers but also on eliciting specific actions and responses to very specific needs, problems, places and circumstances related to the unreached that the Church needs to act on to advance the gospel among the unreached.

So mobilization is more broadly oriented, focused on the big picture of missions, while advocacy is more focused on specific problems, places, and needs. For example, while a mobilizer might try to get a believer to grow in a biblical worldview of global evangelization and the state of the unreached, an advocate would try to get the believer to really care about and act in a specific way in behalf of a certain area of need, a particular mission field, or mission team, or a specific church planting project among the unreached.

Another difference between the two is that Advocacy as a Great Commission role often focuses on engaging with the 'power and hierarchy' to bring about changes in policy, structure and organizational values that are favorable or sympathetic to Great Commission vision and participation. Advocates are the bridges between unreached, those working among them, along with their needs and the Body of Christ.

Advocates seek to influence local churches, ministries or other kinds of corporate structures to give attention to and/or prioritize the Great Commission. The major goal of advocacy is to bring the Great Commission into focus where it wasn't present previously and to alter or remove structural hindrances, much of which is achieved through persuasion, especially of those who are capable and well placed to make these things happen. For example, an advocate may seek to influence the financial policy of a church or ministry to start or increase budgeting for the Great Commission and missionaries. They might want to see a local church or ministry become more active and engaged in the Great Commission through influencing the leadership.

A. The Goals and Purposes of a Great Commission Advocate Include:

1. Seek to change policy in favor of the Great Commission

2. Target systems and structures that prevent or obstruct the interests of the Great Commission

3. Be a voice for an ignored, forgotten or marginalized area of Great Commission interest with the hope of seeing more interest and greater levels of engagement.

B. Some Areas Particularly Suitable for Great Commission Advocates Are:

1. Ministry vision: influencing a church/ministry to embrace a greater Great Commission vision and deeper commitment to the Great Commission.

2. Budget and allocation of financial resources: seeking to see greater financial commitments being made by the church or ministry toward mission.

3. Personnel: encouraging the raising, training and sending of message bearers by the church.

4. Structures and systems: helping to develop appropriate church or organizational structures to enhance Great Commission involvement in a practical way.

Chapter VII.

Welcoming

The Welcomer is a Great Commission role that is starting to gain a lot of attention and popularity now. The major reasons for the rising interest in this role appear to be such issues as the record-breaking enrollment of foreign or international students at local universities around the world; the worsening crisis of refugees crisscrossing the world fleeing from wars and persecution; economic migrants; etc. The world is now witnessing unprecedented levels of both voluntary and involuntary

Most of these people come from poorer and/or desperately unreached parts of the world seeking asylum or wanting to get further education to learn a new skill, among many other reasons.

Often, they come from countries where there is no freedom to share the Gospel, and many have never previously heard a clear Gospel message in their lives. Here, they are in a new country seeking a new beginning, better education, safety and economic security. Welcoming, therefore, sees these kinds of people as a community offering a Great Commission opportunity. As the name implies, it is all about establishing and nurturing friendships with people, whether they are in a refugee camp, an asylum facility, on a university campus, or across the street in a neighborhood. Believers build honest relationships and develop trust, while being a light and witness to the Gospel. Welcomers aim to make these nationals from cultures and countries other than theirs feel welcome, less threatened, and to find a home away from home.

A. Some Ways to Be an Effective 'Welcomer' Include:

1. Open your home to a foreign national to live with your family or stay for a few nights, maybe weekends.

2. Invite them to meals or socials in your home or at your church.

3. Visit them in their own homes or residential areas.

4. Start a group for the internationals within your reach.

5. Volunteer to teach English.

6. Organize local tours to familiarize them with the different places in town, such as malls, markets, places to hang out, etc.

7. Make effort to learn a few basic phrases at least of their language and practice those with them. Every Believer with a Role to Play

GLOBAL MISSION MOBILIZATION INITIATIVE

" The Lausanne Committee for World Evangelization enthusiastically affirms the work and vision of GMMI. GMMI's commitment to mobilizing & equipping the global church toward its role in the task of reaching the world for Christ is compelling and strategic. "

GlobalMMI.net / info@GlobalMMI.net

>>> **Who We Are:** We are a growing global mission mobilization initiative multiplying national mission mobilization movements mobilizing and equipping local ministries and disciples at every level of the body of Christ.

>>> **What We Do:** We multiply local ministries and disciples for the Great Commission in three primary ways:
1. An international step by step strategy multiplying mission mobilization movements at every ministry level across a national church.
2. A Great Commission Equipping Center (GCEC) in Chiang Mai, Thailand
3. A publishing arm, IGNITE Media, producing high quality mission mobilization and equipping materials and resources.

>>> **Core Objectives:**
1. Movements of individual disciples mobilized and equipped for Jesus' Great Commission
2. Movements of individual local ministries mobilized and equipped for Jesus' Great Commission.
3. Movements of individual denominations and church organizations mobilized and equipped for Jesus' Great Commission.
4. Movements of national evangelical alliances and associations in every nation mobilized and equipped for Jesus' Great Commission,

Other Resources From IGNITE Media

IGNITE Media is the publishing arm of GMMI. Books, booklets, bible studies, DVD's, blogs and more are produced to serve your ministry in deepening the spiritual life and mobilizing and equipping for cross-cultural missions.
Visit http://www.GlobalMMI.net/resources/

Cultivating Abandoned Devotion To Jesus

God is calling His people into deeper relationship with Himself. This is the beginning of all effective ministry and the only way effective ministry is continuously sustained. We cultivate this wholeheartedness through studying His Word deeply while applying all we are learning. These Bible studies go deep into the heart of God's Word, revealing depths and insight that will revolutionize your

- Studies in the Life of Joseph
- Studies in the Book of Jonah
- Studies in the Book of Colossians
- Studies in the Sermon on the Mount
- Studies in Jesus' Parables of
  the Kingdom (Matthew)
- Studies in the Seven Churches of
  Revelation
- Studies in Matthew 24 - 25 Jesus'
  End-Times Discourse

Mobilizing Local Ministries

The Holy Spirit is raising a vision of not merely one by one mission mobilization, but the concept of mobilizing and equipping whole local ministries for Jesus' Great Commission. These resources enable that process through the use of proven tools and teaching. Each of these resources serve a unique purpose toward seeing disciples mobilized and equipped through local ministries to serve the unreached.

39

- Handbook for Great Commission Ministries (English, Spanish, French, Chinese (both simplified and traditional), Thai)
- Great Commission Bible Studies
- Global Prayer Teams
- Six Roles in the Great Commission
- Developing a Sending Strategy
- Waking the Giant
- Where's Your Haystack DVD

Equipping For Global Harvest

To see the literal fulfillment of the Great Commission we need to be equipped in particular areas often not discussed or emphasized. These resources provide focus on core areas of equipping the Holy Spirit is emphasizing and that need to be carefully grasped and integrated into our lives if we will be effective.

- Engaging the Holy Spirit
- Declare His Glory Among the Nations
- Proclaiming the Kingdom
- Spiritual Equipping For Mission
- Deeper

www.ingramcontent.com/pod-product-compliance
Lightning Source LLC
Chambersburg PA
CBHW071753020426
42331CB00008B/2298